THE ART OF CHANGING

The Art of
CHANGING

YOUR PATH TO A BETTER LIFE

SUSAN PEABODY

CELESTIAL ARTS
Berkeley | Toronto

Celestial Arts
Box 7123
Berkeley, California 94707
www.tenspeed.com

Distributed in Australia by Simon and Schuster Australia, in Canada
by Ten Speed Press Canada, in New Zealand by Southern Publishers
Group, in South Africa by Real Books, and in the United Kingdom
and Europe by Airlift Book Company.

Cover and text design by Lynn Bell, Monroe Street Studios

Library of Congress Cataloging-in-Publication Data on file with the
publisher.
1-58761-240-2

Printed in the United States
First printing, 2005

1 2 3 4 5 6 7 8 9 10 — 10 09 08 07 06 05

TO MY FAMILY

Those who were;

Those who are; and

Those who are yet to be.

TO THE SEEKERS

Answer the door,

When you hear the knock.

It will be a faint sound,

Somewhere deep within your heart.

CONTENTS

CHANGE IS TO HUMAN LIFE WHAT THE
METAMORPHOSIS IS TO THE CATERPILLAR; IT
IS THE INEVITABLE CYCLE OF LIFE. IF THERE
IS NO CHANGE, THERE IS NO LIFE.

—JOURNAL ENTRY 2003

PREFACE

For years I taught a self-help course called Addiction to Love. At the end of the class I always passed out a list of self-help books. Inevitably, at least one student would raise her hand and say, "I have read most of these books and they don't help. I don't know what I'm doing wrong." Speaking to these students after class, I often discovered that they were stuck because they didn't understand one fundamental truth—our lives don't get better when we read a book or go to a class; our lives get better when we put forth the effort to change.

Is change important? Yes! It is a natural process from which we get a feeling of self-worth and well-being. Unfortunately, sometimes the natural process of changing gets interrupted—usually because we are flung into survival mode by difficult circumstances. This was certainly true for me. By the time I was thirty-two years old, I had not grown emotionally or socially since my adolescence. My maturation had become fixated. I was a creature of habit, not a human being. I was lonely and out of control. I hurt others and I hurt myself. Yet, despite all the pain I was in, I was afraid to change. I was terrified of the unknown.

When my therapist asked what was holding me back from getting better, I said, "I'm afraid to get well. Mental health is unfamiliar. It's a mystery that lies beyond a closed door, and I have no peephole. That mystery feels like a beast ready to devour me if I open the door. What if getting better is worse than being sick? It can happen. Besides, I think I've bonded to my vision of myself as a victim. I prefer self-pity to self-esteem."

This honest appraisal of myself was the beginning of my own personal transformation, which has culminated in this book. While it is meant to be a self-help book, it is also, in many respects, the story of my life.

Why have I written this book? I have written it because I love to teach. I only wish the woman I am today could reach back in time and teach the young woman I was. I would try to help her see what is so clear to me now. That change is important. That there is nothing to be afraid of. That dreams come true if we change. That it is never too late to change, and the sooner we get started, the easier it is to adjust to the changes we make. Most of all, that we are not alone as we make these changes—there are what Joseph Campbell calls "invisible hands," which come to our aid when we are ready to change.

—SUSAN PEABODY
BERKELEY 2004

INTRODUCTION

There are thousands of self-help books on the market. We have more information about the human psyche than ever before. This is the age of self-awareness. In addition, we now have a variety of solutions to our problems. Unlike the first generation of self-help books, any current psychology book worth its salt offers a recovery program that, if followed, will eliminate whatever problem we have.

Despite all of this information, many people still get stuck. They are unable to implement a recovery program. They either can't get started or they can't stick with it, and professionals have a hard time explaining this. We know that the inability to change has a lot to do with personality type, timing, childhood wounds, and the nature of the problem one has to change, but we still cannot completely analyze or explain why people get stuck. I think this is why the art of changing is such a neglected topic. It's a mysterious process, and no one really has any definitive answers as to how to get started and how to stay motivated.

While I don't have all the answers either, I do believe it's time to focus more attention on changing because changing is the bridge between your problems and the solutions. It is your path to a better life.

In Alcoholics Anonymous, members like to say about themselves, "Give us a rut and we'll furnish it." When I first heard this, I had to laugh and say to myself in a reverent way, "Amen to that." If this little attempt at humor strikes a chord with you as well—read on.

A PERSONAL JOURNEY

Years ago, at the end of my last visit with my therapist, she turned to me and said, "Susan, you have a great capacity to change." Then she gave me a hug and sent me on my way. At the time I thought: Is this it? Is this all she has to say at the end of a five-year relationship? Of course, later I came to realize that her comment was the highest compliment she could have paid me. After all, the ability to change is something that many people only dream about. It is a commodity often in short supply, and without it life can be anything from boring to tragic.

Soon after this, I began reflecting on the origins of my ability to change. I had not always had this ability. (Perhaps this is why my therapist felt it was important to acknowledge it.) Actually, for most of my life I had been a slave to habit—to the point of being addicted to relationships, food, and alcohol. Some people thought I was hopeless. Then, one day, something shifted inside of me and I entered the world of the living. I began to change. I began to carve out a better life for myself.

How did I go from resisting change to embracing it? In a nutshell, I finally realized that I had to change or continue being miserable for the rest of my life. Once I decided I wanted to be happy instead of miserable (a big step for me), I looked at what was standing in my way and what I had to do about it. I looked at the rewards of changing and I faced my fears. I prayed and I acted. Before I knew it, changing became a new habit to replace the old habit of resisting change. I have been on a roll ever since, and writing this book is just another way for me to expedite more changes. For now, you see, I am intimate with the process of changing. It is my most cherished companion on this journey we call life.

ACTION

If you listen closely when you unlock a safe, there comes a moment when you hear a click and the tumblers finally fall into place. You can't really see what's happening, but your fingers move and it all comes together. The beginning of change is like this. You do something different and finally something clicks. It is all very mysterious. You don't really understand it, but when it happens you know, you immediately open the safe and take out your valuables. In this case, the valuables locked up in the safe are all the wonderful things you will become when you change. And the key to all this is taking action. You don't just sit there and stare at the safe. You do something.

THE PROCESS OF CHANGING

Changing includes both outer modifications of behavior and an inner shift in values and thinking patterns. The changes you make will be based on insights you've gained. When you are ready to change, you should do the easier things first to build up your confidence and then other changes will follow. Success builds upon success. Sometimes inner changes come from outer changes, and sometimes outer changes are a by-product of inner changes.

Here are some suggestions and techniques to help you make changes. I'll elaborate on these in the rest of the book:

- Recognize when you do something you don't want to do. Dwell on this for as long as you need to. Continued awareness is the beginning of change.

- Break down the changes you want to make into manageable pieces. You can make a list if you want.

- Identify and make a list of alternative behaviors.

- Substitute a good habit for a bad one.

- Give yourself encouragement. Use affirmations.

- Seek advice and help from others.

- Join a support group.

- Make a commitment to a friend or support group; verbalization can really help.

- Avoid companions who don't support you.

- Find role models who exhibit the changes you want to make and observe them for as long as you need to.

- Remember: action leads to motivation leads to more action.

- Don't forget that changing is a process; it takes time. Be patient.

- Avoid negative attitudes that inhibit change. The glass is half full not half empty.

- Visualize the results; become goal oriented.

- Work on building your self-esteem.

- If you are a spiritual or religious person and believe in grace, divine intervention, or the power of prayer, then by all means pray for the energy and willingness to take action.

Don't give up, even if change is slow in coming. If you continue to incorporate these techniques into your life, they will help you change.

WILLINGNESS

Willingness precedes change. The question is, Where does it come from and where does it go? No one knows for sure, but there are three major theories. One theory is that willingness is the by-product of a crisis experience. Another theory is that it comes from some benevolent force in the universe—God or a Higher Power. Finally, some people believe that it just happens. One day a person is unwilling to change, and then the next day he or she is ready to move forward.

CRISIS EXPERIENCE

People in 12-step programs call a crisis experience "hitting bottom." It is any experience, or series of experiences, that bring you to the point where you are ready to ask for help and to do something different. This works for very stubborn people who won't change until their life is really a mess and being stuck has turned into what the book of Alcoholics Anonymous refers to as "incomprehensible demoralization." By this I mean that all hope is gone and the person in question is either in a life-threatening situation or so depressed that she or he can barely get out of bed, and may even be suicidal.

Many people in the grips of such a dilemma die. They take their own lives—sometimes slowly through addiction, and sometimes quickly by jumping off a bridge. For others, however, this incomprehensible demoralization triggers a fear of death and then the next move is quite clear. Change or die!

THE SPIRITUAL APPROACH

While we don't really understand spirituality, we can observe the changes that take place in people once a spiritual awakening has occurred. Over the last twenty years, I've seen many people change after such an experience. They are in a miserable rut. They are powerless over their inner compulsions and have no strength to fight back. They habitually act out in self-destructive and life-threatening ways. Then, in a moment of agony, they call out, "God help me," and somewhere deep in their heart they surrender. They admit they are powerless and they ask for help. Then, they feel willing to change, when before they were afraid. They feel as if they are at the start of a glorious new journey and happily move forward. I will talk more about spirituality later.

IT JUST HAPPENS

Some people don't need to hit bottom or to pray for a spiritual intervention. They just wake up one day and feel motivated. Then they take action. We don't understand just how this works, but I have observed it. I always wanted to be one of these people.

STAY FOCUSED
ON YOURSELF

It is very tempting when trying to change your life to focus on changing others. "If only my husband would change," a wife thinks to herself, I will be happy. Unfortunately, changing other people is impossible. We only have the power to change ourselves. Even if we could change others, it would only take time away from the work we have to do to change ourselves.

I once had a client named Laura who was married to Fred, a full-blown alcoholic. Like many codependents, Laura was obsessed with fixing Fred. She just knew her life would be wonderful if only he would get his act together and stop drinking. Laura found pamphlets about getting sober and left them on the coffee table. She made appointments for Fred with more than one therapist. She begged, yelled, screamed, threatened, and cried until she was blue in the face. Nothing helped.

One day Laura heard about a program called Al-Anon Family Groups. Al-Anon is a 12-step support group for the family and friends of alcoholics. "Great," Laura thought to herself, "They will teach me how to make Fred stop drinking." She marched off to her first meeting with high hopes.

To Laura's surprise, Al-Anon was not in the business of sobering up alcoholics. They were there to help Laura cope with being married to an alcoholic. The 12-steps were there to help her face her own shortcomings and to grow and change. Laura resisted this approach at first, but eventually she gave up trying to change Fred and began focusing on herself. She went to meetings every week and found a mentor. She "worked" the steps and followed the advice of others who had walked in her shoes. She detached from her husband's alcoholism and found peace. She began to change. To this day I do not know if Laura is with her husband or not, but I know she is on the right path.

STUMBLING BLOCKS

There are many stumbling blocks to change. They will vary from person to person, and circumstance to circumstance, but we must remove them one by one as they come up. Here are some common obstacles that stand between us and the person we were meant to be.

DENIAL AND DEFENSE MECHANISMS

Many people can't change because they don't want to change. They feel fine just the way they are and adamantly deny that there is anything about them that needs to be changed. Denial is usually a defense mechanism. A defense mechanism is anything we think, say, or do to manage the feelings we want to avoid. Sometimes even our feelings are defense mechanisms against other feelings. For instance, I get angry to avoid fear and blame others for my problems to keep the fear at bay.

Breaking through denial happens when people are ready. Sometimes quietly, and sometimes in the middle of great chaos, they have a moment of clarity. They remember something that someone told them years before, but they were afraid to acknowledge. For some people this will happen when they wake up one morning. For those less fortunate, it will happen as a judge sentences them to a life in prison. During these moments, people will open their eyes and acknowledge the truth about their situation.

Most of the stories I have heard over the years about breaking through denial are what people in Alcoholics Anonymous call "rude awakenings." My favorite is about the Catholic priest who was in denial about being an alcoholic. One day Father Michael had a little too much communion wine and stumbled over to a group of parishioners standing by the door. Unbeknownst to him, there was a reporter there snapping pictures for the local newspaper. As Father Michael tells it, "One minute I was smiling at Mrs. Davis and telling her how beautiful her new coat was, and the next thing I know I had reached out to stroke her breast. Then I heard the camera click and was blinded momentarily by the flash. The next day I woke up with a hangover and a new awareness of my alcoholism."

My son, Karl, also broke through his denial in an unusual way. When Karl was a teenager, he was angry at me for neglecting him. As a result, he became self-destructive. I think, subconsciously, he was trying to punish me. I won't list all of the self-destructive things he did, but I will mention one. In the ninth grade, he stopped going to school. I talked to him about this. I went to endless parent-teacher meetings at the high school. I sent him to counseling. I went to counseling with him. I tried punishing him—even begging. Nothing worked. Every day, I dropped him off at the high school entrance on my way to work, and after I drove away he crossed the street and hung out in the park with his friends.

The low point for me came the day I received both Karl's report card and a letter from the school's Gifted and Talented Education (GATE) program. The report card indicated that Karl had been absent forty-five times and received five failing grades. As a result, he was now a full year behind his classmates. The letter from the GATE program said, "Your son was given an IQ test and it indicates that he has above-average intelligence. Please call our office to discuss his future. We are convinced that he will do well in our college-bound program. He is exceptionally bright." I cried when I read this, but I didn't know what else I could do about this situation.

A few weeks later, I was sitting at my desk at work. Suddenly, the phone rang and a man with a deep voice asked for Karl's mother. "That's me," I replied. "What can I do for you?"

"I am Karl's school counselor," the man said. "I want to talk to you about your son's absences."

"I am glad to hear from you, but I want you to know that I have already tried everything to get Karl to go to school. With these words I began crying and pouring out my heart to this stranger on the phone. "I love my son. I only want what is best for him. But I can't make him do something he refuses to do. God knows I have tried. So, I am going to pray for him and love him no matter what he decides to do with his life. That is all I can do for now."

When I was finished, there was silence on the other end of the line. Then, solemnly, the man said, "Thank you for your time, Mrs. Peabody. I will stay in touch."

Karl's next report card showed a marked improvement in his attendance and grades. I was ecstatic. The following semester Karl was on the honor roll. I couldn't believe the change. For the next two years, Karl continued to work hard. He went to summer school and evening classes at the local adult school to make up the classes he had failed. He was determined to graduate with his class even though I told him that it was all right with me if he graduated a year late.

Halfway through Karl's last semester in high school, he asked me to go to parents' night. I agreed and he squired me around from classroom to classroom introducing me to his teachers. They were all very happy about Karl's improvement.

Before we went home that night, Karl escorted me to a patio adjacent to the school gym. It was a beautiful night. The moon was full and the stars glistened. Karl and I sat down on a wooden bench just enjoying the moment.

We were both silent for a while, and then Karl turned to me with a smile on his face. For a second he hesitated; then softly he said, "Mom you have never asked me why I went back to school. Don't you want to know?"

"Yes," I replied. "I guess I was so happy that I didn't want to question it."

"Well," he said, "I would like to tell you. A while back, I decided to play a joke on you. So I called you at work and pretended to be a school counselor. For some reason, you didn't recognize my voice and so you shared with me your innermost feelings about the problems I was having. What you said saddened me and made me ashamed. Then, suddenly, I knew deep in my heart that I had to do something to make things right. From that moment on, I resolved to do better—for myself and for you. I decided to change."

Karl did change. He graduated from high school with honors with his class. He went on to get a B.A. from the University of California, Berkeley and an M.B.A. from Dominican College. Today he is a successful broker and continues to grow in his own and special way.

PERFECTIONISM

We do not know if perfectionists are born or made. I know I have always been driven by some inner compulsion to do things over and over again until I get them "just right." Something deep within me gets great satisfaction from this. On the other hand, I remember my mother saying, "If it is worth doing, it is worth doing right." Perhaps trying to please her is also a part of my perfectionism. Whether perfectionism is good or bad, I do know it can be a stumbling block to change if we can't move forward because we are afraid of making mistakes. If you struggle with perfectionism, try to treat yourself as you would an eager child who presents you with his first drawing. Would you point out the flaws or would you praise her for the precious gift she has presented to you? Your efforts are just as precious and worthy of praise.

FEAR

Fear is one of the biggest stumbling blocks to change. Most people are afraid of the unknown. Fear usually manifests itself as something else like ambivalence or denial. Fear also sends us all kinds of negative messages like, "What if things get worse instead of better?" "What if I fail?" "What if I succeed and I can't handle the responsibilities?" To deal with your fear, make a decision and move forward. Even if it is the wrong decision, it is better than doing nothing. Moving forward by trial and error is a legitimate way to change. There is an expression that says it better than I could. "Feel the fear and do it anyway."

TOXIC GUILT

Toxic guilt is the unreasonable guilt you feel for things that are beyond your control. Where does it come from? It is usually the legacy of a traumatic childhood. Because of what psychologists call self-referencing, children blame themselves when something goes wrong in their home. There is no logic to this, it is just a fact. Children with undeveloped egos see themselves as the center of the universe and take responsibility for everything. They think, "If mother is angry, then it is my fault. I am a bad person." This leads to feelings of shame and toxic guilt.

This phase of childhood development has a lasting impact on our adult lives. The feelings of guilt live on in our unconscious mind and float to the surface now and then when we least expect them. This gets in the way of change because it weighs us down. It saps our energy and keeps us in survival mode. We have to spend all of our time fighting off the feelings of shame and guilt, and as a result there is no time or desire to change.

To counteract this kind of guilt we must use positive reinforcement. We must counter the free-floating feelings of guilt with an awareness of the truth—that we are not to blame—and then keep reminding ourselves of this truth with constant self-talk until the guilt recedes. Most of all, we must not act on this toxic guilt. For instance, codependents live lives of quiet desperation trying to get rid of this toxic guilt by taking care of people in unhealthy ways. They must stop doing this and erase the toxic guilt to the best of their ability.

ADDICTION

Nothing stands in the way of change as much as addiction. Addiction is all about holding on to mood-altering experiences and dangerous rituals at the expense of change, even when the changes are necessary to save your life.

Addiction can sometimes feel like demonic possession—in the sense that one is possessed by his or her bad habits. In Alcoholics Anonymous, members pray to a Higher Power: "Relieve me of the bondage of self."

Addiction is hard to understand. It is not logical. An addicted person is a slave to the pleasure compulsion. This is a term I coined to describe a combination of what the Freudians call the "repetition compulsion" (which is the mind's tendency to repeat traumatic events in order to deal with them) and the "pleasure principle," which describes the need of the infant to seek gratification. In adults, this would be called the "production of pleasure."

The pleasure compulsion, or the tendency to repeat the same pleasurable experience over and over again, is an attempt to ameliorate trauma. You can see the pleasure compulsion acted out beautifully in the movie *Casablanca*. Ingrid Bergman is feeling the pain of loss, and it makes her feel better to hear a certain piano piece played by Sam. The pleasure compulsion prompts her to wistfully say, "Play it again, Sam."

Of course, not everyone has the pleasure compulsion. Many people who seek pleasure to dissipate anything from sadness to boredom will move on to other mood-altering experiences—they like variety. Others, however, like routine, and for them, the pleasure compulsion can get out of control. Take the child who is rebuffed by her classmates and eats a cookie to comfort herself. The next morning she wakes up and remembers the pain of being rebuffed. She could do a variety of things to distract herself from the sadness or shame, but for some reason this child remembers how good the cookie tasted and she makes her way to the kitchen. Trauma, pleasure, and repetition become locked. Not just trauma and pleasure; that wouldn't lead to addiction. It is the repetition factor that can change this child's life forever. If it's strong enough, she could end up a food addict.

The pleasure compulsion is seductive, and it may be linked to the desire for control. There is no trial and error necessary when doing something for the second or third time. Whatever worked before is guaranteed to work again—or so we think. Unfortunately, many mood-altering experiences become a magnet for problems. Food lovers get overweight. Heavy drinkers get DUIs. Gamblers lose their paychecks. Then there is the increased tolerance phenomenon. It takes more and more of the experience to get the desired effects—more food, more alcohol, more trips to Vegas. This is the nightmare of addiction. The mood-altering experience becomes a problem, but you are unable to give it up. You're hooked.

It goes without saying that you must remove whatever stumbling blocks there are between yourself and your ability to change. As Wayne Dyer puts it in his book *Your Erroneous Zones*, if we are not growing, we are dead.

FACING YOUR SHORTCOMINGS

To begin the process of changing, you must pinpoint what has to be changed—the exact values, thoughts, and behavior that have to be modified or eliminated. With this in mind, I recommend that you make a personal inventory of your "shortcomings" or a list of the things you want to change about yourself.

There is more than one way to do an inventory. I recommend that it be written, but you may talk into a tape recorder if you prefer. You can make your inventory in marathon fashion over the course of a weekend, or you can take daily notes as you observe yourself doing the things you want to change.

Whatever method you use to prepare your inventory, remember to be as thorough and honest as possible. Consider exploring the relationship between your bad habits and the wounds of your childhood. You need to remember that it is not how you do an inventory that counts, but the fact that you do it. Taking action is the key to changing.

MAKING CHANGES
STEP-BY-STEP

I can't say it enough: Change is a process. First, you identify what needs to be changed. Then you think about it a lot until you crave the willingness to change. When the willingness comes, you decide what has to be changed first. Then, like most of us, you will probably keep doing the same thing anyway. But now, you are fully aware (sometimes for the first time) of what you're doing after you've done it. Then you are fully aware of what you're doing as you are doing it. Then you are fully aware of what you're about to do before you do it. Then, one magic day when you're about to do something you don't want to, somewhere, deep inside of you, you find the courage not to do it. This is it. You have changed your behavior, and in so doing, changed yourself, and the rest of your life from this moment on. Congratulations!

Until I was thirty-two years old, I was always unhappy, but I didn't want to admit that I needed to change. I wanted the world to change, not me.

Eventually, after years of being addicted to relationships, food, and alcohol, I had a nervous breakdown and had to take a good hard look at myself. At the time, I was suicidal, but something deep within me struggled to survive. I think it was the part of me that had not yet been born and wanted a chance to live if only I could change.

When I was finally able to admit that I was the problem, not other people, I got stuck there for a while and just wallowed in self-pity. Fortunately, I had some wonderful people in my life who helped me understand that if I was the problem then I was also the solution. This was good news, because I had the power to change myself, whereas I couldn't change other people.

Eventually, at the suggestion of a friend, I sat down and took stock of the things about myself that were getting in my way. I discovered a lot about myself by doing this task. I found out that at one time or another I was capable of being selfish, angry, dishonest, gluttonous, afraid, resentful, envious, vengeful, intolerant, codependent, mean, lazy, impatient, controlling, demanding, judgmental, blaming, and quick to attack people who disagreed with me.

When the truth was out, I immediately got depressed. But I did not give up and eventually some mysterious force from deep within pushed up from my unconscious and provided me with the willingness to at least dream about overcoming these problems. As Jim Manley puts it in his hymn "Spirit," "from the bondage of sorrow, the captives dream dreams."

When I was ready to change, the first action I took was to select one single thing from the list of things that I wanted to change about myself. Then I made a commitment to overcome this problem. What I chose to change was my bad temper.

I began by breaking down this huge problem into manageable pieces. I chose one manifestation of my temper and decided to work on that first. What I chose was my habit of yelling at my son. I chose this because at a therapy session with my son, the therapist said to him, "If you could change one thing about your mother, what would it be?" My son replied, "I'd like her to stop yelling at me when she gets upset."

To begin trying to change this bad habit, I spent the next few weeks thinking a lot about yelling. I asked myself why I yelled. The answer was that I was frustrated when my son didn't do what I asked him to do, and this was the only way I could get his attention. Then I asked myself what other choices I had. I came up with a plan that I called "calm persistence." The day after committing to this plan, I screamed at my son. Afterward I was overwhelmed with a sense of how easy it was to do something that I had told myself I wouldn't do. However, I didn't give up. I kept trying, and after each failure I spent some time thinking about how the incident had gotten started and how it had escalated.

A few weeks into this great adventure of trying to change, I asked my son to do the dishes when he came home from school. I got home from work expecting a clean kitchen. When I saw the dirty dishes piled up everywhere, I turned red with anger. I was ready to pounce on my son. Fortunately, he wasn't home so I had some time to think about the commitment I had made to calm persistence.

When my son came home, I began talking to him calmly. When he started getting defensive and making excuses, I suddenly found myself yelling at him again. However, this time, instead of feeling as if I was in some kind of trance with no control over the situation, I found myself observing myself as I was yelling. I also felt, for the first time, that I had a choice. I knew I could stop if I wanted to. I used this new sense control to change my behavior. I stopped yelling at my son in midscream and walked out of the room.

Later, despite my small victory, I still felt as if I had failed to reach my goal and I started crying about it. The sobs continued for quite a while and afterward I felt as if a big weight had been lifted off my shoulders. Then I recognized that at least I was thinking about yelling at my son before and during the act—not just afterward. I was making progress.

The next time my son forgot to do the dishes, I talked calmly to him about it and insisted that he do them before going out or turning on the television. He resisted and I persisted—but I did not yell. Afterward, I felt so good about myself for not yelling. This victory lifted my self-esteem and later became a motivation to continue fighting my urge to yell.

From this point on, despite periodic relapses, I continued to have a sense of choice about my yelling rather than feeling powerless about it.

After a year had passed, the urge to yell at my son disappeared, and it seemed normal to handle things without losing control. I still got angry, but I had gotten control over my behavior and I felt better about myself. Most of all, in changing my behavior I had improved my relationship with my son. We were closer and he respected me more. Because he respected me more, he was more cooperative.

Over the years, I have continued to change many things about myself—from hurtful behaviors to small vices. I give myself all the time I need to change, and I never give up. I do *something* even if it's just thinking about the problem and keeping the goal of change firmly entrenched in my conscious mind.

THE POWER OF
THE GROUP

For many people, changing requires working hard with the helpful guidance of others. This guidance can often be found in support groups.

Why do groups help? Honesty is very fragile. It begins to fall apart in isolation. To guard against the withering away of the progress you've made, it's important to find a community of other people who are also working to change. Many wonderful things happen in such a place:

- You'll tell your story out loud and find out, to your amazement, that you are not the only one with this problem and that you are not banished from the group.

- You'll find love and support from others who really understand what you're going through.

- You'll find strength you didn't know you had and the hope you thought you had lost.

- You'll find more wisdom about how to change than you know what to do with.

- You will find a place where you can be honest and share secrets. This will help dissipate your toxic shame.

- You'll learn a lot about your problems and what you can do about them. The people you meet will share their insights and recommend books and other resources. This will facilitate the changes you want to make.

- You'll be reminded to guard against procrastination and denial, because showing up is a constant reminder that you need to change.

- Calling people in your support group will help you avoid the dysfunctional behavior that you want to change. You can call someone before acting out in some irrational way.

- Support groups make you accountable to the group. You'll find yourself doing for them what you can't do for yourself. (As you develop your own inner strength, accountability to the group will become less important.)

Of course when looking for a group you need to take some time to find a good fit. Some people will benefit from a therapeutic approach and should look for a professionally facilitated support group. The therapist in such a setting will keep things on track and provide the kind of structure some people need to feel safe. Usually these groups work best for people who just need a jumpstart and not a lifetime of support.

If you are looking for a spiritual solution, and think a long-term support network is beneficial, you will find 12-step programs very helpful. Twelve-step programs, like Alcoholics Anonymous, believe that there is a benevolent force in the universe that can do for you what you cannot do for yourself. Even within the category of 12-step programs, however, you need to look around until you find a group that feels right. You will know it when it happens. Sometime during the course of the meeting you will have a sense of homecoming.

I was lucky. This happened to me in 1982 at my first 12-step meeting. I really didn't think my problem was out of control, but I sat there as someone explained how the program worked. Then, something the moderator said caught my attention. "You will have to learn how to ask for help," she announced. "Not me," I said to myself. "I don't need anybody's help." As the meeting continued I listened attentively. Then, at some point, I began to have a feeling of homecoming. I could not explain it, but I felt as if I was in the right place—that I had come home after a long journey. I started crying and in embarrassment I turned my face to the wall. The woman next to me raised her hand and said, "How do you know you belong here?" "You just know," I whispered to myself. "You just know."

THE POWER
OF THERAPY

Some people move easily beyond a difficult childhood and just naturally make peace with it. Others will have to really explore what happened to them because they are haunted by the past. In her book *The Drama of the Gifted Child*, Alice Miller puts it this way:

> Experience has taught us that we have only one enduring weapon in our struggle against mental illness: the emotional discovery of the truth about the unique history of our childhood.... In order to become whole we must try, in a long process, to discover our own personal truth, a truth that may cause pain before giving us a new sphere of freedom. The damage done to us during our childhood cannot be undone, since we cannot change anything in our past. We can, however, change ourselves.... We become free by transforming ourselves from unaware victims of the past into responsible individuals in the present, who are aware of the past and are thus able to live with it. (Alice Miller, *The Drama of the Gifted Child*, p. 1)

Therapy is a mixed bag. Sometimes you have a good therapist and you get a lot out of it. Sometimes you have an inadequate therapist and it's a waste of time. But, nothing ventured—nothing gained—and if you're not satisfied with your progress in your support group, then giving therapy a try might do the trick. The individual attention and intuition of a therapist can untangle a lot of mysteries. And change always begins with the truth.

Of course, therapy is a slow process, especially if you just sit there and talk. What makes therapy work is acting upon the insights you get from a good session. Furthermore, your therapist is not going to wave a magic wand and change you. *You* have to do the work. One day I told my therapist that I was unhappy with the progress we were making. "What do you mean *we?*" he said. "Well," I mumbled, "isn't this a team effort?" "No," he said, "You're the one who has to do the work. I hold the flashlight; you chop the wood."

I was shocked by this statement, but it was the beginning of a change in my attitude about therapy. I realized my therapist wasn't going to fix me. I had to start doing things differently if I wanted to change. The following story explains how therapy helped me change.

As long as I could remember, I had been angry with my mother— both as a child and as an adult. Once I had a dream in which I was so angry at my mother that I was paralyzed. I couldn't move. I opened my mouth to scream at her, and the words got stuck in my throat. Later in the dream I was talking to my father, and he told me that my mother was pregnant. I went into a rage. Then my mother appeared and I screamed at her, "You are going to do to another child what you did to me?" I was so angry I woke myself up.

I didn't tell my therapist about the dream right away. Instead I went to my mother. I wanted to process my feelings about my childhood with her, so I asked her a lot of questions about what was going on in the family when I was young. Mom just stared at me. She didn't want to talk about it. "I don't remember," she said. I was livid. Not only had she neglected me as a child, and exposed me to the parent who had abused her, now she was impeding in my attempts to get better.

When I finally talked to my therapist about it, he said something interesting. He shrugged his shoulders and said sympathetically, "Oh, she couldn't do it." I stopped dead in my tracks when I realized that he didn't say "she *w*ouldn't do it." He said she "*c*ouldn't do it." What a difference a letter can make. I suddenly began looking at my mother in a brand-new light.

It took time, but eventually I changed my mind about my mother. A change in my feelings quickly followed. Then I started treating my mother differently. I changed. Our relationship changed.

This is how therapy is supposed to work. You uncover things. You process your feelings. Your feelings change. You treat people differently. You change. Your relationships change. Then you repeat the process all over again.

HEALING THE WOUNDS OF THE PAST

Healing the wounds of the past begins with changing how we look at it. I had a friend, Megan, who hated how her apartment looked so she never had any company. Rather than change how the apartment looked as a way to change how she felt about it, she just complained. The thing she hated the most was her couch. It was a gift from her mother, but she hated it. Every time she looked at it she got angry or depressed. She thought about giving it away, but that didn't seem right either. She grew up watching all of her favorite television shows on this couch. One day Megan decided to put on a new slipcover. Suddenly, the couch looked different. It looked bright and cheerful. The next thing you know Megan was cleaning her whole apartment and buying new furniture to go with the couch. This made her feel like inviting her friends over for a party. One of her friends brought her brother Fred with her, and he asked Megan out for a date. One thing led to another and Megan and Fred got married. Now they are very happy together with the couch and all the furniture he brought with him from his apartment. Our past is like this couch. Give it a new look and move on with your life.

While changing how we look at the past is a very important part of change, this is only one piece of the puzzle. In analyzing it closely, I've come up with the following summary of the healing process, presented in the form of actions you can take. Don't get stuck on one particular aspect, just keep pushing forward.

1. Identify the things that happened to you.

2. Talk about them.

3. Write about them.

4. Feel your feelings fully—no matter what they are or how afraid of them you are.

5. Accept what has happened to you.

6. Accept what you did in reaction to what happened to you.

7. Forgive those who hurt you.

8. Forgive yourself if you passed your anger on to others.

9. Try to find something good that came out of all the chaos.

10. Move on. Live in the moment.

The trauma of my past began with my childhood. It consisted of neglect, abandonment, peer rejection, covert incest, prolonged illnesses, and the death of my brother. This left me with a lot of anger, anxiety, shame, and fear, as well as low self-esteem and a tremendous hunger for love. As I was growing up, I didn't understand that I had been traumatized. I just knew that something was wrong with me. I knew that pain and emptiness kept reappearing in my life whenever I wasn't being distracted by one of my addictions.

As an adult, I became accustomed to the pain and adopted it. In its own way it comforted me. Then, before I knew it, self-pity was my best friend. I was, for all intents and purposes, a misery addict. To keep myself wrapped in this blanket of self-pity, I put myself in situations that caused me, and others, a lot of pain. By others, I mean my parents and my children.

When I first began to look at this, I was in denial about the trauma I had suffered in my family of origin and the misery I had inflicted on myself and others. I remember recognizing that the prolonged ridicule I had suffered at school hurt me a lot, but when I thought about my family I remember them being very normal. Of course, I was in denial. Years of therapy would reveal the truth about how I was affected by my father's alcoholism and my mother's depression. As for my victim mentality, that was really out of reach. No one could tell me I had perpetuated my own misery. That was absurd. Then there were the people I had hurt. When a person feels like a victim all the time, they don't see the people they have hurt. This was certainly true for me.

Eventually, after my life fell apart, I began to face all of this, which was an important step for me. Then, when I was ready, I investigated the past by talking to my family and other people who knew me when I was growing up. As a result, the pieces of the puzzle slowly came together and a picture emerged of an unhappy, neglected child caught up in a dysfunctional environment that had been passed down from generation to generation. Next, I did an inventory of what I had done as an adult to perpetuate the pain of my childhood. Then I looked at what I had done to hurt others—like a wounded animal lashing out in pain.

Once I broke through my denial and identified what had happened to me and what I had done to myself and others, I began talking about it. At some point, I also began writing about what had happened. However, I was still unable to *feel* very much at this point, so my writing was very analytical. This was my way of recognizing the pain but not feeling it.

After some time, the dam burst and all of my painful feelings about the past came rushing forth. At first I was angry. Then I was overwhelmed with sadness. For me, these feelings would come and go, but every time I discovered something new, or I realized how much I had been wounded in the past, I faced my feelings and had a good cry. I cried a lot.

Eventually, I moved on from my feelings and addressed the issue of acceptance. Acceptance was a very important part of the healing process for me. It is a tool I learned in 12-step programs. It doesn't change the basic situation, but it ends our struggle against things that can't be changed, leaving more energy to focus on the things that can be. Acceptance amounts to surrendering your pain so that you can move on. You just give it to God or some benevolent force in the universe and in return you get the serenity you need to heal your wounds. To get started I recommend the first half of the very popular Serenity Prayer: "God grant me the serenity to accept what I cannot change."

PARENTING
YOURSELF

When I was growing up I was very headstrong. It was difficult for my parents to discipline me, so they gave up trying. Interestingly enough, this lack of discipline made me feel unloved. I remember wishing I had some of the restrictions that my friends moaned and groaned about.

Because no one restrained me, I didn't know how to restrain myself, and my lack of self-discipline eroded my self-esteem. I always felt out of control and ashamed of myself. I used to beg my mother to give me the structure I needed. She would shrug her shoulders and say, "I can't make you do anything you don't want to do."

Furthermore, both of my parents were clinically depressed and addicted to mood-altering substances. As a result, they didn't have the emotional energy to give me the love and nurturing I needed. Throughout my childhood, my mother was very withdrawn. It took all of her energy to provide for the physical needs of our family. Furthermore, my mother didn't like me. She told me once that I reminded her too much of her mother—who of course was a terrible person.

Like most children, when I couldn't get what I needed from my parents, I looked for it elsewhere. This began a lifelong pattern of looking for love outside of myself. It never once occurred to me that I could love myself.

As an adult, I was introduced to the concept of self-parenting (or reparenting) in a support group. Self-parenting is a therapeutic approach to healing the wounds of our childhood. It is an attempt to give ourselves now what we did not get as children.

The "inner child" is a term adopted from a concept introduced by Eric Berne in his book, *The Games People Play: The Psychology of Human Relationships*. In his book, Berne introduces the world to Transactional Analysis—a revolutionary new way of looking at the human psyche. Later Thomas Harris in his book, *I'm OK, You're OK*, popularized this idea. The child ego state eventually became the "inner child," which in turn led to a series of popular books: Hugh Missildine's *Your Inner Child of the Past*; Charles Whitfield's *Healing the Child Within*; John Bradshaw's *Reclaiming and Championing Your Inner Child*; Philip Oliver-Diaz and Patricia O'Gorman's *Twelve Steps to Self Parenting*; and Cathryn Taylor's *The Inner Workbook: What to Do With Your Past When it Won't Go Away*—just to name a few. Over the years the concept of the inner child has been both applauded and trivialized, but it is still an important tool to help us finally grow beyond a state of arrested development.

When I first heard about self-parenting, I was excited about what it offered. I recognized that part of my personality that embodied an emotionally undeveloped little girl who felt unloved and ashamed of herself. Up to this point I had never really had a concept of myself this way. I had been told by my friends that I could "act like a child," and I knew that I was wounded, but it never occurred to me that I could heal this part of myself by getting to know my inner child. Suddenly I was excited about giving my inner child the love and benevolent discipline that she had been denied years before. I also knew that loving my inner child would help me focus on changing myself rather than trying to change others.

I met my inner child in an unprogrammed meditation. I got into a comfortable position and closed my eyes. Then I let my mind wander until my little girl appeared to me. In my meditation we were in a park together. She had an angry expression on her face, but I could sense the pain and sadness that lay beneath her anger. I called to her, but at first she refused to come near me. Eventually, however, she slowly walked toward me. When she was finally close to me, I reached out and stroked her hair. She immediately broke down and cried. I took her in my arms and began rocking her back and forth. I reassured her. I told her I was here to be her mother. I promised to give her everything that she needed to feel loved and safe.

Since then, I've continued to develop a relationship with my inner child as a way of learning to love myself. Today, this relationship is threefold: I love and comfort my little girl (Susie); I set limits with her; and we play together. As a result, she has, for the most part, stopped acting out, and her pain no longer permeates my life. She is content and no longer needs mood-altering experiences to anesthetize her pain. Most of all, my self-parenting has helped me grow up, and this maturation has paved the way for other changes.

BUILDING
SELF-ESTEEM

Low self-esteem hinders change. It saps people of the energy and courage they need to change. It also traps them in what I call "survival mode." There is little room for thoughts of self-actualization (becoming the best person you can be), which requires taking risks, when you're consumed with protecting what little self-esteem you already have.

The origin of low self-esteem is unclear. It's hard to know whether children are born with a natural feeling of self-worth and then sometimes lose it, or whether some children are born without it and never get a chance to develop it. Either way, low self-esteem is a painful disorder. It can be seen as both a mental and a spiritual wound.

Even if children are born with a natural reservoir of self-esteem, they need to be validated by the people around them if they are to build on that sense of self-worth. Love and attention are the most important forms of validation. Unfortunately, children don't always get enough love and attention.

As well as finding themselves unloved, many children are also neglected, abandoned, and sometimes abused. This causes children to unconsciously assume that something is wrong with them. They don't want to believe that the adults around them are bad—this would be too frightening—so they conclude that they themselves are bad or flawed. If they believe they are flawed, then they assume they are worthless. If they believe they are worthless, then they feel unworthy of love. The end result of this unconscious chain of logic is low self-esteem.

There isn't always a direct relationship between the degree of neglect or abuse and level of self-esteem, but usually, the more children are neglected or abused, the less self-esteem they have. However, this isn't the only factor to consider when trying to determine the impact of neglect and abuse on self-esteem. The level of sensitivity children are born with and any insulation they might have had while growing up also impact their self-esteem.

Once a child has low self-esteem, this mind-set begins to feed on itself. Because of their poor self-image, such children are incapable of compensating for neglect and abuse by loving themselves. They are also unable to accept the small of doses of love their parents do provide, or the love of other people they may meet as they are growing up. This triggers more shame and low self-esteem, in turn producing other painful emotions and conditions, such as:

- Chronic insecurity

- Chronic anxiety

- Depression

- Feelings of alienation

- Loneliness

- A profound hunger for love

- Exaggerated fears of abandonment and rejection

- Feelings of deprivation

- Feelings of emptiness

- Confusion or fear when love is available

- Anxiety when things are going well

- Addiction

- A lack of ambition

- A fear of people

- Self-loathing

- Self-destructive behavior

All of these feelings and conditions hinder change. Therefore, if we attack the problem of low self-esteem, we free ourselves to change.

I first heard the expression "low self-esteem" at a support group in 1982. One of my friends said, "Susan, I think you have low self-esteem." "What does that mean?" I asked. "That means you don't like yourself," she replied. I didn't know what to say. I had never really thought about whether or not I liked myself. I didn't even know it was important to like myself. When I thought about it, I realized she was right. I didn't like myself. So, I decided to go searching for self-esteem. You might say I was "desperately seeking Susan." Little did I know how much finding self-esteem would help me grow and change.

I began my quest by reading a lot of books and magazine articles about self-esteem. This promoted my self-awareness and kept me focused. My favorite book was *Celebrate Yourself*, by Dorothy Corkill Briggs.

Reading helped me understand that my low self-esteem was related to my childhood. When I was growing up, I took my mother's lack of attention as an indication that something was wrong with me. The teasing of my classmates reinforced this negative attitude. Their voices eventually became my inner critic.

To counteract my inner critic now that I was an adult, I began affirming myself—consciously thinking nice things about myself. I told myself that I was a worthy person despite my shortcomings. I also made a list of my attributes and began focusing on them. In effect, I was trying to brainwash myself. It worked a little, but there was still more work to be done.

I have always felt that intimacy comes from revealing ourselves to a nonjudgmental person. The combination of acceptance and knowing is a powerful one. It naturally follows, then, that to love myself more I not only had to accept myself, I had to know myself better.

I began trying to get to know myself better by making a list of all the things that I liked and disliked. I also read a book about personality types and found out which one I was. Then I looked at my values—my code of ethics. As the weeks passed, I spent time alone with myself. I talked to myself. I reread the inventory I had made of the things I wanted to change about myself. I explored my feelings when they came up. I began dreaming about my future. I remember asking myself, somewhat facetiously, "Susan, what do you want to be when you grow up?" (I wanted to be a writer, by the way.) In general, I stopped focusing on other people and spent more time focusing on myself. In so doing, I developed a friendship with myself that I continue to enjoy today. And it *is* easier to esteem myself now that I know who I am.

I have always been a perfectionist. I don't know if I was born with a preprogrammed sense of order, or if I just wanted to be perfect to get my parents' attention. I do know, however, that I have always been ruled by an inner mandate to do everything just right, and that this perfectionism eventually became a hindrance to my self-esteem. In other words, I could only feel good about myself if I could do something perfectly. Eventually, I came to realize that this attitude was a trap, because human beings cannot be perfect. We are perfectly imperfect. We always live in the shadow of perfection. I also began seeing my perfectionism as arrogant, as well as impossible, and how it eroded my relationships with others because it was so tied in with my need to control. To deal with this, I lowered my standards and decided to settle for being human. I started giving myself credit for things like showing up, doing my best, making progress, and so on. Giving up my all-or-nothing attitude boosted my self-esteem.

While I had to give up perfectionism, I couldn't feel good about myself unless I lived up to some reasonable standards. This is where my self-respect comes from. Therefore, I had to begin incorporating some reasonable self-discipline in my life. This meant giving up my addictions. I knew I couldn't be totally out of control and have high self-esteem.

At first, I thought the idea of earning self-respect contradicted the idea of self-acceptance or loving myself unconditionally. However, I finally decided that, because of the complexity of human nature I did need to find some balance between the two. So, today, I expect to put forth some effort in order to engender self-respect, but I also love myself when I fall short.

Over the years, my low self-esteem often manifested itself as a lack of self-care. I neglected my appearance, and I found it impossible to do anything nice for myself. Instead, I focused all of my time and energy on doing nice things for others and making sure my children looked good. Somehow, I knew this was eroding my self-esteem, but I didn't know what to do about it.

Eventually I came up with a plan. I decided that since we take care of what we value, it only makes sense that we will learn to value what we take care of. So I began taking care of myself and doing nice things for myself even though I didn't feel as if I deserved it. I stopped spending all of my money on others. I took time to pamper myself. I even learned how to be selfish now and then. It was difficult, but once I got used to it I started to like it, and it had a tremendous impact on my self-esteem. I started to feel like a genuinely valuable person.

I not only started taking better care of myself, I also let other people do nice things for me. I gave up my monopoly on giving. I stopped dismissing compliments and returning gifts (so I could use the money to buy gifts for others). I let the love of others come in, even though this made me feel uncomfortable at first because deep down I was afraid to be loved—it was too new and different.

As part of my new self-care, I also started setting limits with people who were trying to take advantage of me. In other words, I started standing up for myself. This meant learning to say no, expressing my own opinion, walking away from abuse, being assertive when appropriate, and no longer apologizing when I hadn't done anything wrong. Reading books about codependency helped me understand why I found it so difficult to do these things, and once the pattern became obvious, it went on my list of things I wanted to change about myself.

At some point in my recovery, I went to a workshop about self-esteem. The teacher said that high self-esteem was linked to altruism. She said people feel good about themselves when they are generous and charitable. I questioned the teacher after class, because all of the nice things I had done for people over the years hadn't helped my self-esteem. The teacher didn't have an answer for me, but after I thought about it, I came to realize that altruism has to be balanced with self-care. It also has to be freely given. All the giving I had done over the years had been motivated by an attempt to buy love. Therefore, to a certain extent, my generosity had been contaminated by my own neediness and less-than-pure motivations. As a result, helping others didn't build up lasting self-esteem, it was just a quick fix. After I realized this, I decided that I would only give to others when I could do so with a free heart—with no strings attached. Also, I decided to always combine my altruism with self-care. You might say I decided to love my neighbor as I love myself—no more, no less.

Another bad habit that eroded my self-esteem was comparing myself to others. Instead of loving who I was, I always wanted to be someone else. I looked at my friends and envied their success, and my envy always cast a dark shadow on my own life, keeping me from feeling good about myself. So I made a real effort to stop comparing myself to others. I have been somewhat successful in doing this, and it has helped my self-esteem.

I believe strongly that creative people have high self-esteem. I know that when I started writing and sharing my work with others, I began to feel really good about myself. I wrote poems to my family instead of buying them birthday cards. I started writing in my journal so that my children would someday be able to see into my heart and soul. I started teaching about addiction at a local adult school and writing articles about codependency for my students. As I got better at writing, people thanked me for my efforts. Before long, I was compiling my class notes into a book that was eventually published. By using my creative energy instead of hiding it under a bushel, I was not only allowing the world to see me and validate my budding talent, I was being who I was born to be. This made it much easier to love myself. It's hard to love our false self or our undeveloped self—that part of us that is lost in the wilderness of addiction or caught up in survival mode and afraid to change.

While self-love comes from within, I am only human, and I do need some human validation. Unfortunately, before I knew better, I tended to choose companions who did not validate me. They abused me in the same way that my classmates had abused me when I was a child. I finally realized that, although I didn't have a choice about the people who surrounded me when I was a child, as an adult I am free to choose my friends and lovers. It only made sense to choose people who affirm me. So I started doing this.

Unfortunately, when it comes to family and coworkers we can't always choose our companions. We can move from job to job or just ignore our family, but I didn't want to do that. So instead, I learned how to stop taking my family and coworkers so seriously. I learned how to filter out inappropriate criticism or counter it with positive self-talk. This got easier over time, and today I'm much less sensitive to what other people think of me. As a result, I have the ability to protect my newfound self-esteem.

Nothing can be substituted for the warm feeling of self-esteem. It brings a subtle kind of happiness that's hard to describe. Because it's linked with confidence, it provides the courage we need to face our fear of changing. And with the absence of fear, there is one less stumbling block to the natural process of changing.

Amazing Grace

In my first book, *Addiction to Love*, I discuss the relationship between spirituality and change. Today, I still believe that there is a benevolent force in the universe that can transform us if we cooperate. This process is mysterious. No matter how much we speculate and write about the topic, we still do not know how it works. To me it does not matter how spirituality works. I do not know how my car headlights work, but I turn them on when it gets dark so I can see my way down the road.

For those who want to give spirituality a try, and see for themselves if it helps them change, try one or more of the following spiritual disciplines.

12-STEPS TO A BETTER SPIRITUAL LIFE

1. Meditation: Get quiet and listen to God through your feelings and intuition.

2. Prayer: Talk to God (out loud or in your head) as if you were talking to a close, personal friend.

3. Humility: God is a higher power. You are a lesser power. You know this. You are humbled by it.

4. Study: Read, write, learn, listen.

5. Simplicity: Slow down. Experience and appreciate the simple things in life—nature, music, and friends.

6. Solitude: Take some time to be alone and listen to your own inner music. Putter around your nest.

7. Submission: Surrender everything to God—as you understand God.

8. Service: Reach out to people in need and give of yourself and your resources.

9. Confession: Find someone you can trust and confide your deepest, darkest secrets to them. Release the shame.

10. Worship: Be in awe of your Higher Power. Bow your head—metaphorically or literally. Be thankful for the grace that has been freely given to you.

11. Celebration: Be grateful! Raise your hands in joy and celebration. Sing, dance, and be merry.

12. Guidance: Work with a mentor who is in constant contact with God.

I had no idea that there was any relationship between spirituality and change when I first discovered God. I was just hanging out in a 12-step recovery program trying to go with the flow. Prior to being in the program, I had not thought much about God. As far as I was concerned, God had given birth to us and then died leaving us to fend for ourselves. But my addictions had humbled me, and I was trying to be open-minded. This in itself was a miracle.

At the time, I was surrounded by spiritual people and they were constantly advising me on the subject of spirituality. One close friend suggested that I surrender myself to God even before I had fully come to believe in the reality of a Higher Power. I thought this was a ridiculous idea, but I decided to give it a try anyway. So I memorized a prayer in which I surrendered to God. I also prayed for God to reveal himself to me. I repeated this prayer often and waited to see what would happen.

One day as I was sitting with my support group and silently praying, I began to feel a warm glow all over my body. Then a sense of peace fell over me, and all of my fears disappeared only to be replaced by great joy and happiness coupled with a complete confidence that God really existed.

From that point on, not only did I believe in God's existence, I knew that I could have a personal and loving relationship with him (or her). This was a special experience for me. After a lifetime of confusion, doubt, and apathy about spiritual matters—not to mention a little contempt—I was meeting God for the first time. I had knocked on the door and God had opened it.

After the joy and peace of that moment receded (it has never completely left), I felt like a different person. Almost immediately, I could tell that my desire to change had been given a big boost. Changing no longer felt like a chore; it felt like an opportunity. I was full of energy, excitement, and courage. I wanted with all of my heart to be a better person.

This new excitement about changing was accompanied by other gifts from God that promoted my growth, such as more patience and an intuitive sense of what I needed to do to change. My spirituality also acted like a magnet drawing in information. I met people who would tell me exactly what I needed to hear. Books practically dropped off the library shelf into my lap. Joseph Campbell describes this manifestation of spirituality when he says that invisible hands will come to our aid when we are on the right path.

My new relationship with God also had an impact on my self-esteem. I had never realized before that God loves me. Once I got to know God, however, his love poured over me and dissipated the remnants of my self-hate. Building self-esteem got a lot easier after that.

I wish I understood more fully the relationship between spirituality and change. But I don't think I ever will. I just accept it as a mysterious phenomenon—a gift.

TREATING
DEPRESSION

Depression acts like a wet blanket smothering the desire to change. It makes people tired and apathetic. It saps them of enthusiasm and the energy they need to change. You might say depression is like a thief in the night. When you wake up in the morning you have been robbed of the desire to do anything but the mandatory and routine things you need to do to survive.

Clinical (biological) depression is a chemical disorder and can often be corrected with antidepressants. Emotional depression often needs talk therapy or a dose of cognitive therapy, which is outlined in Dr. Burn's book, *Feeling Good*.

Depression has to be dealt with. Even more than fear, perfectionism, denial, or low self-esteem, it can pin us to the ground and make it impossible to change.

I have suffered from depression since I was eight years old. I can see the pain on my face in old photographs of myself taken while I was growing up. Over the years, I used mood-altering experiences, such as eating, getting drunk, and falling in love, to ease the pain. Eventually, these experiences stopped working and the depression overwhelmed me. I became suicidal.

When I got into therapy and joined a support group, I felt better. As I worked through childhood issues, began to love myself, and found the joy of spirituality, the pain eased and I thought I would never be depressed again.

Then, in 1990, I was struck down with a debilitating depression. It came out of nowhere. I didn't understand it at first, but every day when I woke up in the morning I cried because I didn't want to face the day. I didn't know what was happening.

I went back to therapy and tried to do more grief work. I continued my reparenting. I also pushed myself to go to my support group and to show up at work. The depression grew worse, and eventually the pain was so bad that I wanted to die. I was tired all the time because I couldn't sleep. My appetite went away, and I lost a lot of weight. Eventually, my body was under so much stress that I broke out in hives. I was covered with huge welts. The hives worsened, and my eyes and lips became hideously swollen. Then the histamine under my skin turned bloody. Steroids helped a little, but nothing took away the problem.

Eventually, I collapsed from all of the stress and my doctor sent me to see a psychopharmacologist—a psychiatrist who approaches emotional disorders with drugs to correct abnormal or faulty body chemistry. I remember getting a minor traffic ticket while driving to his office. I started crying and couldn't stop. When I arrived at the therapist's office I was a mess.

I was prepared to talk about my problems with this new therapist. However, he didn't want to hear the story of my life; he just wanted to ask me some questions. I answered them, and he looked at me with great tenderness in his eyes. He said, "Susan, I believe your problem is chemical. I don't think talk therapy is going to help you this time."

The doctor then gave me an article about clinical depression. I resisted the idea of being clinically depressed, although my family had a history of this problem. I absolutely did not want to take medication because both my mother and sister had become addicted to narcotics prescribed by a doctor. (Later I learned that they had become addicted to painkillers in an attempt to mask their depression.)

Because I was afraid of medication, I suffered for a few more weeks. Then, one day I couldn't stand it anymore. With tears in my eyes, I called my doctor and agreed to give the medication a try.

If the medication had not worked so quickly, I would have suspected that my condition had improved on its own without intervention. However, within days of taking the medication, I was sleeping through the night. The hives disappeared and I came alive again. I was not high, I just felt good because my body was not in so much pain. And I was ready to go back to growing and changing.

Today, I understand depression in all its many forms, and I realize that different kinds of depression require different treatments. I also understand that depression is the enemy of change and must be worked through in one way or another.

FORGIVING OTHERS

> FORGIVE: TO GIVE UP RESENTMENT OF OR CLAIM TO REQUITAL FOR; TO CEASE TO FEEL RESENTMENT AGAINST (AN OFFENDER); TO STOP BLAMING OR BEING ANGRY WITH (SOMEONE) FOR SOMETHING THEY HAVE DONE.
> —MERRIAM-WEBSTER DICTIONARY

Some people believe forgiveness is important and others don't.

In his book *Alcoholics Anonymous*, author Bill Wilson (the cofounder of AA) discusses forgiveness and says it's necessary for sobriety. He calls it "letting go of resentment," not forgiveness, and says it's not done to please others, but in the interest of self.

Resentment is the "number one" offender. It destroys more alcoholics than anything else. From it stem all forms of spiritual disease, for we have been not only mentally and physically ill, we have been spiritually sick. When the spirituality malady is overcome, we straighten out mentally and physically.... It is plain that a life which includes deep resentment leads only to futility and unhappiness.... [T]his business of resentment is infinitely grave. We found that it is fatal.... If we were to live, we had to be free of anger.... They [resentments] may be the dubious luxury of normal men, but for alcoholics these things are poison. (pp. 64–65)

On the other hand, there are the scientific psychologists (as opposed to the transpersonal therapists), like Susan Forward, in *Toxic Parents*, and Ellen Bass and Laura Davis, in *The Courage to Heal: A Guide for Women Survivors of Child Sexual Abuse*, who proclaim that forgiveness is not necessarily a part of the process of changing—it might even be dangerous. In talking about recovering from an abusive childhood, Susan Forward says this:

You may be asking yourself, "Isn't the first step to forgive my parents?" My answer is *no*. . . . [It] is not necessary to forgive your parents in order to feel better about yourself and to change your life.... Why in the world should you "Pardon" a father who terrorized and battered you, who made your childhood a living hell? ... Early in my professional career I too believed that to forgive people who had injured you, especially your parents, was an important part of the healing process.... The more I thought about it, the more I realized that this absolution was really another form of denial.... One of the most dangerous things about forgiveness is that it undercuts your ability to let go of your pent-up emotions. How can you acknowledge your anger against a parent whom you've already forgiven? (pp. 187–189)

The question is this: Is it possible that Bill Wilson and Susan Forward are both right? Yes. Susan Forward is correct when she says that we must own our anger. Anger is honest. Anger in the right setting is therapeutic. Anger can lead to justice. Anger can free us from tyranny. And by coming out against forgiveness, Forward allows us to take our time without shame. Bill Wilson, in my opinion, is also right. If we stop resenting people, we feel better about ourselves and others. This changes us and our lives. This is why I believe forgiveness is the ultimate goal no matter how long it takes.

If you decide that forgiveness is for you, it might be helpful to realize that letting go of anger does not mean you have to like the person who hurt you or continue to let that person persecute you. Actually, you don't even have to be around people who hurt you if you don't want to. For years I attended a church where another member absolutely hated me. I loved to talk about my involvement in 12-step programs, and she was so narrow-minded that she spoke up against me. "I am tired of hearing about those steps," she used to say. One day she berated me at a committee meeting and I quietly left. I went home and wrote a letter to the pastor tending my resignation on the committee. I ended the letter with the lines, "You know, Christ asks us to love our neighbors and our enemies alike, but some people you just have to love from a distance."

Furthermore, forgiveness is not a constant state. It ebbs and flows like the tide. Sometimes you feel good about those who hurt you, and other times you feel the anger all over again. But this doesn't mean you have not progressed. I've found that, as long as I ask God for the strength to release my anger, or announce it in my support group that I am going to "turn it over," or tell my therapist I am really tired of these resentments and want them to go away, the anger comes less and less often.

Please note, despite my own personal feelings about the value of forgiveness as a therapeutic and healing device, and the right moral choice for me, I feel strongly that it is a very personal choice and that people should not be told to forgive when they're not ready. They shouldn't be shamed by others, and they should not shame themselves. They should just push themselves gently in the right direction.

HOW HAS FORGIVENESS CHANGED MY LIFE?

Years ago, I wrote my mother a letter offering her my forgiveness. When she received the letter she cried (since I had asked her not to call me, my sister phoned to tell me). It was almost six months later that my mother went into the hospital for emergency surgery. As I sat by her bed in the recovery room she reached out and took my hand. Tears started streaming down her face, and she said, "Susie, you will never know how much your letter meant to me. I love you so much." I started crying too and we just sat there in silence—the wounds healing and the peace settling into our hearts.

This was the beginning of my lifelong attempt to let go of the past and forgive all the people who had harmed me. After Mom, everyone else was a piece of cake. Interestingly enough, after forgiving my mom for her shortcomings, I also found it easier to forgive myself for the mistakes I had made with my own children.

FORGIVING
YOURSELF

As I mentioned earlier, there's another obstacle to change that most people don't think about—the guilt and shame they feel for hurting others. They get so caught up in these feelings that they lack the motivation to move on. Many people can't even get started because of this burden. Fortunately, there is a solution to this age-old problem—forgiving yourself.

To begin forgiving yourself, it's important to accept the fact that you're not perfect. Embrace your humanity and the fact that you make mistakes. The resulting humility is necessary for change.

Please note that making amends means more than just an apology. If you're rude to someone in the grocery store, maybe saying you're sorry is enough, but if you are rude to a friend all the time, making amends means offering your friend a new relationship—one in which she or he is no longer being hurt.

If you have some serious amends to make, for what 12-step programs call "wreckage of the past," making them will be harder than you think and won't always take the course you want or expect. Still, it must be done if you are to change.

I had a really difficult time forgiving myself for neglecting my son Karl and my daughter Kathy. Even as I write this I feel a lot of guilt. However, since recognizing what I did to them I have apologized and made what they call in 12-step programs a "living amends." This means doing now what you would have done then if you could go back in time. With my daughter Kathy this process took on new meaning when she decided to have children, and little did I know when she got pregnant that I would soon have an opportunity to make a significant amends to her and begin to forgive myself.

In 1994, Kathy got pregnant. I was ecstatic. I wanted very much to be a grandmother and have a second chance at parenting. I knew Kathy and her husband Monty would make good parents and that the cycle of dysfunction would be broken by them.

Early in June, three months before she was due, Kathy went into labor and did not even know it. She thought she was having a back-ache. By the time Monty rushed her to the hospital the baby's little foot had started to come out. The doctor said that if the delivery could be delayed just two weeks the baby would have a chance. We prayed. We begged God. Monty even dreamed the baby would wait. On June 16, 1994, at 11:04 P.M., Jasmyne Marie Snyder was born. She weighed one and one-half pounds. Monty was too nervous to be in the operating room (Kathy had a cesarean), so I was there when little Jasmyne came out. She was perfect.

We watched over Jasmyne for fourteen days while she struggled to hang on. During this time, my heart ached for my daughter. The pain was as sharp as a knife. I had to ask God, "Why are you doing this? Kathy does not deserve this. Punish me. I am the one who failed at parenting. Give Kathy a chance to be a mother." The waiting made me sick. Jasmyne sucked in the air of her ventilator. Her little swollen hand reached out to me. When she grabbed my hand it was as if she was pulling out a plug and tears came rushing out of me.

Jasmyne passed away on June 29, 1994. They took her off the ventilator, and we all rushed down to the hospital chapel. Kathy couldn't bear to be there and asked me if I would stand in for her. I was afraid, but I had to do this for my daughter. The doctor, pastor, nurse, Monty, and I all sat side-by-side. We each held her in turn. A moment after she was placed in my arms she stopped breathing. I was the last one to be with her on this earth. Later, Kathy told me how grateful she was. It was at that moment that I felt I had finally made my amends to her, and for the first time I could really begin to forgive myself.

HELPING
OTHERS

Helping others is a good way to help ourselves change. Studies have shown that in cultures where kindness and generosity are valued there is a direct link between altruism and self-esteem, and, as I discussed earlier self-esteem makes it easier for people to change. (If you are codependent, remember to balance this with self-care.)

Helping others is also a wonderful antidote for depression, which gets in the way of change. When I get depressed, I try to find someone who needs help. It distracts me from my own pain and if the person I am helping is in worse shape than I am, everything I am going through is diminished. As my mother used to say, "I cried because I had no shoes until I met a man who had no feet."

Working with others in a teaching capacity is especially important. Teachers, or what 12-step programs call *sponsors*, have to study hard to keep one step ahead of their students. At some point it occurs to them that everything they are trying to teach others about changing their lives for the better can be applied to themselves. Teachers are also role models and often do the right thing just to help inspire their students. As a teacher, I often push myself this way, so my students will respect me. Of course, you do not need to have a teaching credential to be a teacher. Whenever you are offering advice, you are acting in this capacity.

Helping others is the cornerstone of 12-step programs. As you may, or may not, know, 12-step programs began with Alcoholics Anonymous (AA). AA, in turn, began with a meeting between Bill W. and Dr. Bob.

In 1935, Bill was traveling for a business meeting. He felt like drinking after six months of sobriety. To avoid slipping, he called around and found someone to help him. This is how he met Dr. Bob. They stayed up all night and helped each other stay sober. Then Bill realized that the spirituality that had jump-started his sobriety, and was now being tested, was not enough. Reaching out to someone else was necessary to stay sober. This is how AA was born, and all the 12-step programs that developed from these roots have used this tool to promote and solidify recovery.

Helping others is easy. It may mean taking someone under your wing or being a good parent. It may mean giving advice or just listening. It may mean telling someone your story or helping them move. It may mean being a role model. It can be simple or complicated. It can be constant or occasional. Some people get into the helping professions, and others just go visit a friend in the hospital. It doesn't matter how you help others, only that you do it.

CHANGE YOUR MIND, CHANGE YOUR LIFE

Most changes begin with a decision. You decide to think or behave differently. This changes your attitude, which changes your feelings, which changes your life. It is the proverbial ripple effect.

I had a friend who hated the holidays. Every year he complained bitterly. I said nothing. Then one year he had a revelation. He realized that he hated the holidays out of habit. His childhood had been difficult, and the holidays were not a happy time. Now he was grown and there was nothing to be unhappy about. He realized he had options, so he decided to live in the moment and see if there was anything to enjoy. To his surprise, he found a lot to be happy about. What happened to him? He just changed his mind.

AFFIRMATIONS

Some people criticize themselves repeatedly for doing the wrong thing, hoping this will change them. This rarely helps. Instead, it fosters shame and brings only short-term changes, not a long-term transformation. Affirmations are more constructive.

An affirmation is a set of chosen words designed to help you change your thinking patterns, then your feelings, and then your behavior. You memorize affirmations and, if all goes well, they help you change. Affirmations can be short and soothing, like "God loves me," or they can be a statement designed to help change your behavior, such as "Today I am going to be enthusiastic and nice to everyone I meet. Today I am going to make a difference in someone's life." Affirmations help you remember the things that will transform you.

I use affirmations all the time. A few years ago, I used them to deal with my tendency to perceive rejection where it did not exist. This was an old habit of mine. It always came up when I asked people to help me. When they said they were unavailable, my mind always translated this as "They do not care about me; they're selfish; they're rejecting me." Then I felt either hurt or angry. Rarely did I try to look at the situation from their point of view. I was always ready to project my history of abandonment onto anyone who didn't follow my internal script, which was "If I ask for help, drop whatever you're doing and rescue me. Otherwise, you don't care."

Eventually this caught up with me. I had a friend named Karen, and one day I asked her to meet me for lunch to discuss my latest crisis. She said she was busy. At first, I accepted this. Then I ran into her in a shopping mall and I got upset. My internal dialogue went like this: "How can she have time to shop and not help me? I guess she doesn't care. She's just selfish." Then I immediately felt abandoned. This was quickly followed by both anger and sadness.

I went home after this and sent Karen an email telling her how I felt. That seemed like an honest, straightforward way to communicate my feelings. I refused to acknowledge to myself that my words had a tone of accusation because I was angry. Well, she had her view of things—which she promptly shared with me. "You are so needy," she said. Of course, I got defensive, and we traded emails for the next few days—each of us expressing our point of view. I'll spare you the details, but things fell apart after this, and Karen didn't want to see me anymore.

I was distraught after the relationship ended and began to rethink the whole episode after talking to my therapist. Finally, I decided that all of this happened because of my hypersensitivity and tendency to perceive abandonment where it didn't exist. When I brought this up with a friend who knows my history, she suggested several reasons for my neurosis. Right in the middle of her well-intentioned remarks, I said, "This is all very interesting, but I already *know* most of what we are discussing. I want to move to the next level. I want to do something about it. I want to change." My friend smiled and said, "Let's make a list of affirmations." "Do those really work?" I asked. "Well, let's give it a try," she said.

Over the next few hours, we came up with the following list.

WHEN PEOPLE ARE UNAVAILABLE

- No one is purposely trying to abandon or reject me, and I can choose to remember this.

- I don't need to be a hostage taker. I can honor somebody's saying "I am not available."

- How other people spend their time is none of my business, and I will not judge their choices.

- "No" is a complete sentence. I do not have to change people's minds.

- I have enough people in my life that even if someone isn't available to me I'm ok. I have God, other people, and meetings.

- My serenity is not dependent on any one person's availability. I can be serene even if no one is there to help me.

These affirmations worked for me. I read them every day and internalized them. Then, the next time someone was too busy to help me, I felt less abandoned than before. As a result, I didn't react so quickly and act out. Instead, I waited and talked to some friends. Then, what little abandonment I did feel dissipated, and I was able to look at things more clearly. For me, this was a great victory. I had changed.

MENTORS AND ROLE MODELS

One of the ways that babies grow and change is by learning from their parents what to do and not do. If you did not learn these important lessons, and are a bit confused by what to do and not do, I suggest that you find mentors and role models and listen to their advice. Mentors and role models help you because they hold the mystery of how to do what you're struggling to do. They can give you good advice, and if you observe them carefully, they can demonstrate what you need to learn. Interestingly enough, you don't even need to understand how they do what they do. You just need to imitate them and follow their advice until it changes you. "Fake it till you make it," as they say in 12-step programs.

Some of my mentors over the years have been gentle with me. Others were people who disliked me and told me what they really thought of me. After I got over the shock, I thought about what they said, kept the helpful comments, and discarded what wasn't helpful. Then I changed what needed to be changed.

Some mentors came as a surprise and only brought a single lesson. Years ago I used to go into San Quentin with a group of volunteers to participate in a 12-step meeting. I met Michael and worked with him for almost a year. When it was time for him to be released, he came to me to say good-bye. He thanked me profusely, and I could feel my pride welling up. I gave in to the temptation to stroke my ego and said to Michael, "Of all the advice I've given you, what helped you the most?" The moment the words were out of my mouth, I felt embarrassed, but without missing a beat, Michael turned to me with a look of surprise on his face and said wholeheartedly, "I really don't remember much of what you said. I just remember that you kept coming back." It's not the message that saves people—it's the love. This is what Michael taught me.

My daughter Kathy is my best role model. Years ago, when I wanted to change, I began observing her carefully. I noticed that she was a good listener, calm most of the time, patient, polite, and quick to see other people's point of view. Also, she didn't take things personally. We used to call people like her charming and mature. These days we would say she has a great deal of "emotional intelligence." This term, coined by Daniel Goleman in his book by the same name, suits Kathy well. She seems to have been born that way. I know she didn't get these characteristics from me.

Since Kathy is my role model, when we're together I take cues from her. If we're at the supermarket and people are annoying, she stays calm. Every time I start to get upset, I just look at her and think, if she can be polite so can I. When we're apart, I frequently ask myself, "What would Kathy do in this situation?" Then I do it. Most of all, I spend a lot of time observing her interact with people and literally copy her movements. For example, I noticed one day, while watching her, that she spends a good deal of time listening to people. She nodded her head and smiled as they went on and on. Now this was something I rarely did so I decided to give it a try. My list of friends almost doubled. It is rather interesting to have your role model, and the woman you admire most in the world, turn out to be your own daughter. All I can say is that God works in mysterious ways.

THE 12 STEPS

I cannot talk about change without mentioning the 12 steps. Originally developed for alcoholics, they now help millions of people change their lives.

Members of 12-step programs don't just talk about the steps, they do them. They use the term "working the steps" because the steps were designed to give people something to do to expedite change—taking action. Here's that word again—"action"—it is the key to everything.

I talk about the 12 steps in my first book, but what I had to say bears repeating. Here is an updated version of my concept of the 12 steps.

1. *We admitted we were powerless over _____—that our lives had become unmanageable.* This step is designed to help people face the truth. It is about honesty and humility. Don't be afraid of the word "powerless." It simply means that you're admitting you need help. You, by yourself, are powerless. Aligned with the group and a Higher Power, you have the power to move forward.

2. *Came to believe that a Power greater than ourselves could restore us to sanity.* Once again, you are admitting that you need help. By yourself you cannot

change. With some power beyond yourself, you can change. This "power greater than yourself" does not have to be a traditional deity. It can be a group, an idea, a belief system—anything that gives you the strength you need to change. This step is also about hope. Armed with help you can be restored to sanity—you can change.

3. *Made a decision to turn our will and our lives over to the care of God as we understood Him.* All changes begin with a decision. In this step you're making a decision to align yourself to the will of your Higher Power. Your Higher Power may be God or your inner wisdom, but either way you are making a decision to do the will of this Higher Power and not the will of your fear-driven self—your ego, your addiction, your dark side, your immaturity—whatever part of you holds you back from change. Turning your will and your life over simply means surrendering to change.

4. *Made a searching and fearless moral inventory of ourselves.* An inventory is always a good idea. Listing what you like about yourself and what works to help you change is as important as listing the things about yourself that are holding you back.

5. *Admitted to God, to ourselves, and to another human being the exact nature of our wrongs.* Confession is good for the soul. It is an ancient art that has never lost its importance. It is a ceremony in which you graduate from the old into the new. It is part of the process of change.

6. *Were entirely ready to have God remove all these defects of character.* Since willingness is so important for change, you have to wait for it before you can proceed. While you are waiting,

there are some things you can do. You can keep praying or hitting bottom—whatever works.

7. *Humbly asked Him to remove our shortcomings.* If you, by yourself, could remove your own shortcomings you probably would—once you have recognized them as a liability. But the truth is, you need help. If you are humble enough, your Higher Power will help you. This is the message of the seventh step. Swallow your pride and ask for help. "Humbly" means that, with gratitude and faith, you are openly asking your Higher Power, to do for you what you cannot do for yourself. Asking for help doesn't mean you don't have to do your part. There's a great story about a little boy who asked God to fix his toy. Nothing happened, so the little boy got impatient and said, "God, what is taking so long?" God answered, "I will fix the toy as soon as you let go." So if God has not lifted one of your shortcomings, go back to step six. Furthermore, don't expect this step to work like magic. If you pray for patience, you won't suddenly become patient; people who drive you nuts will come into your life so you can practice patience.

8. *Made a list of all persons we had harmed, and became willing to make amends to them all.* As with the fourth-step inventory, once again you are asked to put pen to paper (or hand to keyboard). Make a list of all the people you've harmed. This step prepares you for taking action by taking action. The eighth step is the beginning of letting go of guilt and shame—major stumbling blocks standing in the way of change.

9. *Made direct amends to such people wherever possible, except when to do so would injure them or others.* Making amends is painful, but it's the only way to truly release yourself from the burden

of guilt and shame. Once it's over you will be glad you did it. You will feel, deep inside, how this step has changed you. Remember that when making amends, you only try to clean up your side of the street. The other person's part in all this is irrelevant when it comes to the amends you are making. In the book, *Alcoholics Anonymous*, there's an excellent explanation of how to avoid injuring others when you make amends and when it's better to not make amends at all.

10. *Continued to take personal inventory and when we were wrong promptly admitted it.* Slacking off is a major problem when it comes to change. This step is designed to keep you honest and to help you avoid slipping back into your old ways. Some people do this step daily, others do it only when they've done something they feel badly about.

11. *Sought through prayer and meditation to improve our conscious contact with God as we understood Him, praying only for knowledge of His will for us and the power to carry that out.* This step is for the spiritually inclined. It improves your relationship with your Higher Power. It relaxes you. It reminds you that you shouldn't rely only on your own ego to make life decisions. If spirituality is an important part of your life, this step will keep you on the right path.

12. *Having had a spiritual awakening as the result of these steps, we tried to carry this message to [other sufferers] and to practice these principles in all our affairs.* This step is all about service, which keeps you feeling good about yourself. It suggests you work with others who have problems similar to yours, but I think in its broader sense it means that you get outside of your own problems, and your own ego, and reach out to your fellow human being. Part two of this step is about moving out from

the safety of your support network and into the world at large. You are reminded that the changes you make should be demonstrated not just at your support group or with your therapist but at home and at work.

There are many books written about the 12 steps, and I recommend them all. The steps work whether you do them alone or within a 12-step program. They can help you change more quickly than any other method I have come across.

Progress—
Not Perfection

Changing is a slow process. You have to learn the art of accepting failure while still pushing forward to the next milestone. Accepting failure is easy if you are humble. Humble people understand that they are not perfect and that failure is part of who they are. They also reframe failure and see it as a legitimate part of the learning curve. I, for one, have learned more from my failures than my successes.

When I first experienced the emotional high of being able to change, I assumed I could speed up the process and get rid of all my problems overnight. I started reading virtually every self-help book on the market and really trying hard to be a new person. However, soon I had to face the fact that changing takes time. Improvements come very slowly and are often painstaking.

Today, I'm still changing, and the process is still slow, but I continue to think positive thoughts and wait for that little push from within to do something different. I have weathered some relapses and more times than I care to count crawled back to what they call in 12-step programs "the road of happy destiny." However, I've never given up the notion that I am on a journey and should always be moving forward.

Most of all, I can truly say that today I am not the person I was when I started my metamorphosis twenty-two years ago, and that, God willing, I will always be pushing forward—changing. For it is by changing that I get closer to being the person God always meant me to be.

CONCLUSION

In conclusion, I want to reiterate that change is a natural process that we must not interrupt by clinging to our familiar routine. We must remove any stumbling blocks by little acts of will under the guidance of God or some intuitive force within us that knows what is best. We must root out our bad habits and try new things.

To keep your spirits up, you can keep track of your progress by writing a journal and reading it every few years. In 12-step programs, members are asked to tell their life story every now and then. In the process, it is easy to see how much they have changed. You can also tell your story to your therapist or a trusted friend and make note of how different you are today compared to how you were when you started your journey.

It is also important to celebrate the changes you have made. Addicts pick up chips at 12-step programs. Others can set aside one day a year to celebrate the milestones of their lives. On your birthday, you can take some time to reward yourself for the progress you have made. I recommend that everyone also write their own story. My favorite form of storytelling is the parable. The parable I wrote about my own life was about a woman named Sorrow who met an angel and decided to go on a journey in search of

God. On this journey she met her husband Passion whom she left to find God, only to find out she was pregnant with twins—Comfort and Expectation. She took care of her babies, and when they grew up they left on their own journey. Sorrow continued on in search of God, and after many trials and tribulation she made it to Heaven where she met Spirit, who invited her to go to the Angel school. At her first class, she met her best friend Solitude. After graduating from Angel school, Spirit gave Sorrow the name Beloved and sent her off to help people. (For the full parable, look for "Where Love Abides" on my website www.brightertomorrow.net.)

I really had a lot of fun writing this story, and every now and then I add new chapters to celebrate my life and mark my progress. I encourage you to do the same—to do something significant and fun to celebrate the journey you are on—wherever it takes you. In this way you will be emboldened to make more changes, which, after all, is the path to a better life.

UNIVERSAL WOMAN

Daughter of woman,

Mother of woman:

You are the link

Between past and future.

Woman alone,

Woman among many:

Seek out the truth

Of your own identity.

Child of God,

Sister of mankind:

Let not your mourning body

Deter you from your quest.

Nameless soul,

Wandering in a timeless maze:

Be not afraid

Of your new beginnings.

Universal woman,

Smiled upon by all:

Your wounds will be healed

And you will stride proudly forth.

BIBLIOGRAPHY

Alcoholics Anonymous, Third edition. New York, NY: A.A. World Services, Inc., 1976.

Berne, Eric. *The Games People Play: The Psychology of Human Relationships.* New York: Grove Press, 1964.

Bradshaw, John. *Healing the Child Within, Reclaiming and Championing Your Inner Child.* New York: Bantam Books, 1990.

—— *Healing the Shame That Binds You.* Deerfield Beach, FK: Health Communications, 1988.

—— *Homecoming: Reclaiming and Championing Your Inner Child.* New York: Bantam Books, 1990.

—— *Creating Love: The Next Great Stage in Growth.* New York: Bantam Books, 1992.

Briggs, Dorothy. *Celebrate Your Self: Enhancing Your Own Self-Esteem.* Garden City, NY: Doubleday, 1977.

Burns, David. *Feeling Good: The New Mood Therapy.* New York: Morrow, 1980.

Butler, Pamela E. *Talking To Yourself.* San Francisco: Harper and Row, 1983.

Campbell, Joseph. *The Hero with a Thousand Faces.* New York: Princeton University Press, 1949.

Copeland, Mary Ellen, with Matthew McKay. *The Depression Workbook: A Guide for Living With Depression and Manic Depression.* Oakland, CA: New Harbinger Publications, Inc., 1992

Dyer, Wayne. *Your Erroneous Zones.* New York: Avon Books, 1976.

Forward, Susan. *Toxic Parents: Overcoming Their Hurtful Legacy and Reclaiming Your Life.* New York: Bantam Books, 1989.

Gillett, Richard. *Change Your Mind, Change Your World.* New York: Simon and Schuster, 1992.

Goleman, Daniel. *Emotional Intelligence.* New York: Bantam Books, 1985.

Harris, Thomas. *I'm OK, You're OK: A Practical Guide to Transactional Analysis.* New York: Harper and Row, 1969.

Hauck, Paul. *Overcoming Frustration and Anger.* Philadelphia, PA: Westminister Press, 1974.

Jeffers, Susan J. *Feel the Fear and Do It Anyway.* San Diego, CA: Harcourt Brace Jovanovich, 1987.

Johnson, Spencer. *One Minute for Myself.* New York: Morrow, 1985.

Kidd, Sue Monk. *God's Joyful Surprise: Finding Yourself Loved.* (Christian literature) San Francisco: Harper and Row, 1987.

Larsen, Earnie, and Carol Larsen Hegarty. *Change is a Choice.* Center City, MN: Hazelden Educational Materials, 1992.

May, Gerald, G. *Addiction and Grace:
Love and Spirituality in the Healing
of Addictions*. San Francisco:
HarperSanFrancisco, 1991.

Miller, Alice. *The Drama of the Gifted
Child*. New York: Basic Books,
1996.

Missildine, W. Hugh. *Your Inner Child
of the Past*. New York: Simon and
Schuster, 1963.

Nakken, Craig. *The Addictive
Personality: Roots, Rituals and
Recovery*. Center City, MN:
Hazelden, 1988.

Oliver-Diaz, Philip, and Patricia A.
O'Gorman. *The Twelve Steps to Self
Parenting for Adult Children*.
Deerfield Beach, FL: Health
Communications, 1988.

Peabody, Susan. *Addiction to Love*.
Berkeley, CA: Celestial Arts, 2005.

Pearson, Carol. *The Hero Within*. San
Francisco: Harper and Row, 1986.

Peck, Scott. *The Road Less Traveled: A
New Psychology of Love, Traditional
Values, and Spiritual Growth*. New
York: Simon and Schuster, 1978.

Reynolds, David. *Playing Ball on
Running Water*. New York: Morrow,
1984.

Rosellini, Gayle, and Mark Worden.
*Here Comes the Sun: Dealing With
Depression*. Center City, MN:
Hazelden, 1987.

Sills, Judith. *Excess Baggage: Getting Out
of Your Own Way; Overcoming the
Blind Spots That Make Your Life
Harder Than It Has to Be*. New
York: Viking Press, 1993.

Smedes, James B. *Forgiving and
Forgetting*. San Francisco: Harper
and Row, 1984.

Solomon, Andrew. *The Noonday
Demon: An Atlas of Depression*. New
York: Simon and Schuster, 2002.

Sonkin, Daniel. *Wounded Boys, Heroic
Men*. Stamford, CT: Longmeadow
Press, 1992.

Taylor, Cathryn. *The Inner Child
Workbook: What to Do With Your
Past When it Won't Go Away*. Los
Angeles: Jeremy P. Tarcher, 1991.

Wegscheider-Cruse, Sharon. *Learning to
Love Yourself*. Deerfield Beach, FL:
Health Communications, 1987.

Wholey, Dennis. *Becoming Your Own
Parent*. New York: Doubleday,
1988.

Williamson, Marianne. A Return to
Love.

Wright, H. Norman. *Making Peace with
the Past*. Old Tappan, NJ: Revell,
1985.

Personal Inventory

ABOUT THE
AUTHOR

Susan Peabody has been writing professionally since 1985. Her first book, *Addiction to Love: Overcoming Obsession and Dependency in Relationships,* was published by Ten Speed Press in 1989. A third edition was published in 2005. For more of Susan's writings see her website: brightertomorrow.net.